french sign language

french sign language

READING COMPREHENSION ACTIVITIES

D. L. Ellis
M. R. Pearce

NATIONAL TEXTBOOK COMPANY • Lincolnwood, Illinois U.S.A.

In the same series:

German Sign Language
Italian Sign Language
Spanish Sign Language

This edition first published in 1988 by National Textbook Company,
4255 West Touhy Avenue, Lincolnwood, Illinois 60646-1975 U.S.A.
© D. L. Ellis and M. R. Pearce 1975. All rights reserved. No part of
this book may be reproduced, stored in a retrieval system or
transmitted in any form, or by any means, electronic, mechanical,
photocopying or otherwise without the prior written permission of
National Textbook Company.

Manufactured in the United States of America.

8 9 0 ML 9 8 7 6 5 4 3 2 1

PREFACE

The main purpose of this book is to provide students of French with reading material for comprehension. It contains one humdred and ten photographs of everyday signs and notices readily visible in French towns.

The most obvious place for a visitor to France to be faced with reading is in the street: on walls, windows, kiosks and vehicles; and in buildings or at camp sites. Failure to observe and understand the information or requests on display may lead to unnecessary inconvenience, embarrassment or, even worse, injury to people.

We read our own language for pleasure, or to refresh the mind, or to gain information. While some people may develop their reading skill sufficiently to read French for pleasure and to refresh the mind, many of us will probably never want to do more than read to gain information.

French sign language is primarily designed for students of French who wish to apply their reading skill to the basic realities of life outside the classroom. It could also be used to form the language content of any course in exploratory French.

D.L.E.
M.R.P.

CONTENTS

TEACHER'S NOTES

Grading of material

The photographs are roughly graded according to the amount of reading matter containe in them. The first photographs contain only two or three words, whereas those at the end o the book convey information in twenty or more words. No attempt has been made to grou the photographs according to subject matter, in the belief that their random order reflects the way in which the reader would come across these signs in France. Teachers wishing to plan lessons according to situations may refer to page 63 for a list of topics.

Exploitation of material

The technique used for exploitation is basically the same throughout the book: the student is asked in English to react to the reading matter in each photograph. In some instances, the context is briefly described before the reader is asked to demonstrate com- prehension of the printed word. In other instances, the reader is confronted with the readir 'task', put into a particular situation, and asked either to decide on the necessary course of action to achieve a given objective, or to make the correct inference. It should be emphasis that it is not the intention to provide a set of comprehension tests, but a series of exercises which constitute at the same time a basis for teaching and discussion.

Selecting photographs for a lesson

In the case of a teacher wishing to allot part of a lesson to **French sign language,** perhaps once a week, it is suggested that a limited number of photographs be selected for exploitat The photographs may be chosen from any part of the book according to the needs of the class: selection may depend on the vocabulary items or language patterns contained in the photographs, on the subject matter or on the difficulty of the reading.

Vocabulary and language patterns

It is suggested that before the lesson the teacher will have ascertained that the vocabular at the end of the book is sufficiently explicit to enable his particular students to understan the language of the photographs to be studied. The French-English vocabulary offers trans- lations appropriate to the context for most of the legible words in the photographs. Excep- tions are words whose meanings the average reader might reasonably be expected to guess correctly, and words not relevant to the exploitation offered or of only secondary import- ance. Complications such as gender of nouns and endings of verbs and adjectives have been kept to a minimum in the belief that fuller information is not required for comprehension. The forms shown in the vocabulary are those found on the actual photographs. Inevitably, the accents on some of the signs are missing or incorrect; this may need some explanation.

Since reading comprehension is a receptive or passive skill, it will be readily appreciated that the language content of the photographs is not intended for internalisation and active production. Hence, in the main, the word list consists of items intended for passive recognition only. Even if the development of rôle playing is envisaged (see *Further possibilities* in these notes), the active vocabulary expected of pupils should be limited to the basic requirements of the situation. The list of question patterns (page 10) and the notes on rôle playing (page 11) provide an indication of the level suggested.

Should an explanation of any of the language patterns in the selected photographs be considered necessary, it is recommended that the teacher clarify such points by resorting to the use of parallel examples. A list of language patterns contained in the photographic material, with references to specific photographs, is to be found on page 64.

Classroom activities

In all instances, the comprehension work may, if desired, be done orally in the first place, and then as a writing activity. On the other hand, students may be required to work alone, at their own speed from the outset, writing down their responses as a quiet learning experience. It is recommended that students be told clearly how fully they are expected to write their answers, and to what extent they ought to justify them. The teacher may prefer answers to be in the form of complete sentences or simply one-word responses where appropriate. When the comprehension activity has been completed by the class, students could be asked to check each other's work. At this stage, the teacher could take the opportunity of discussing matters arising from the answers, thereby helping to increase the students' knowledge of the French way of life. Discussion concerning the French way of life, however, could equally well precede the comprehension activity.

Further possibilities

In addition to the basic comprehension and response activity in English, it is possible to exploit further the photographic content of *French sign language* for oral work in French. Having understood the information conveyed by a photograph, some students will clearly benefit from answering questions in French on visual details which may or may not be directly related to the reading matter.

The questions chosen should of course be of the type which visitors to France may need to ask. They should also be of the type which visitors, who have to fend for themselves, are likely to be asked. A list of useful questions could be prepared by the teacher before a class is introduced to the book, and then appropriate questions chosen from the list for oral work with each photograph. In this way, over a period of time, each type of question may recur many times so that a stage will be reached where students gain real oral skill, albeit within a limited range of question and answer patterns. Students should similarly reach a stage where they are able to initiate the questioning procedure. Depending on the needs of the students, this type of oral activity may be followed by appropriate written work. In any event, this writing activity may be found to assist students gradually to reinforce oral skills.

The set of question patterns which follows, although not exhaustive, is designed to be of help to those teachers who are interested in devising their own list of useful questions, for the purpose described above, and who will wish to take advantage of a check-list.

Vous désirez?
Qu'est-ce que vous désirez?
Qu'est-ce que vous voulez?
Avez-vous (quelque chose)?
Vous avez (quelque chose)?
Combien coûte (quelque chose)?
Ça fait combien?
Où allez-vous?
Où est (quelque chose)?
Où se trouve (quelque chose)?
À quelle heure . . . ?
Quand est-ce que (quelque chose se passe)?
Est-ce qu'on peut (faire quelque chose)?
On peut (faire quelque chose)?
Où est-ce qu'on peut (faire quelque chose)?
Pour (faire quelque chose) où faut-il aller?
Pour (faire quelque chose) qu'est-ce qu'il faut faire?
Y a-t-il . . . ?
Est-ce qu'il y a . . .?
Il y a . . . ?
Voulez-vous (faire quelque chose)?
Vous voulez (faire quelque chose)?
Aimez-vous mieux (quelque chose) ou (quelque chose)?

Alternatively, it is seriously suggested that English responses to questions, requests or instructions in French should be considered acceptable proof of both listening and reading comprehension, bearing in mind that the responsibility of having to produce a foreign language has an inhibiting effect on some students.

Students who have become used to the comprehension activity in English, and the oral exchange in French, based on a pre-determined core of question and answer patterns, may further benefit from simple rôle-playing work. A given photograph will suggest its own rôle-playing dialogue to the teacher.

Rôle-playing may be between either pupil and teacher, or pupil and pupil (pairs work). For example, taking photograph 60 as the situation, one pupil could play the part of an English tourist who has pulled off the road here, while the other (or the teacher) that of a French *gendarme.* The *gendarme* should inform the tourist that parking is forbidden on that date. The tourist should apologise and ask where he is allowed to picnic. The *gendarme* supplies the information requested.

Or, taking photograph 101 as a basis, the pupil could be given a shopping list and asked to buy as many items as possible in accordance with the advertisements. The teacher, or pupil, could play the part of the Co-op assistant.

If these examples are thought too complicated or difficult, almost any photograph can form the basis of simpler work. For example, using number 3, a pupil could be required to stop a passer-by, and ask if he might drink the water.

It should perhaps be emphasised that efficient communication, rather than accuracy, is the aim in such work. Also, where the teacher plays one rôle, it should be that of the native speaker. The pupil takes the rôle of the tourist or visitor, and is required to initiate communication and to react to language of 'native' quality.

D.L.E.
M.R.P.

Notices such as this present few problems to English-speaking travellers, as the meaning of the information is obvious. Notices in two or more languages are often displayed at sea ports and air terminals in order to help foreigners. However, once you leave the terminus, you are not likely to find signs conveniently written in English.

Imagine that you are now in France. During your stay, you are likely to come across many signs and notices similar to those in this book. See how well you can understand what they are about. Incidentally, you will notice that a number of accents are missing or incorrect; some French people can be rather careless about them.

french sign language

A car driving past this sign would **2** probably be going at walking-pace. It might also have to stop several times. Why?

You are camping and want water for cooking and drinking. Do you get it from this tap, or not?

3

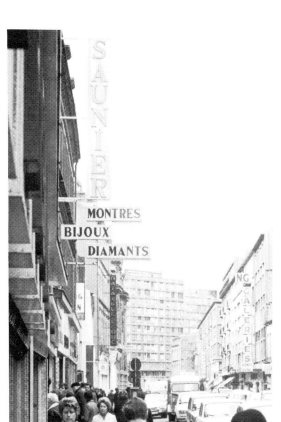

If you were rich enough, what presents could you buy at Saunier's to take home?

DOUCHES

4

You are at a camp site. If you needed to go through the door bearing this sign, would you most probably be carrying:

- a) a bag of rubbish?
- b) a blanket?
- c) soap and towel?
- d) a shopping basket?
- e) some cutlery?

5

This sign is particularly important for British drivers visiting France. Why? What risk do they run?

You are in a coach following this post office van. Does the notice in the rear window warn your coach driver: **6**

- a) that it has air brakes?
- b) that it might be stopping at any moment?
- c) that it has an insecure load?
- d) that the driver is under instruction?
- e) that it is on tow?

You are visiting a seaside town. If you wanted to go from this point to the beach, would you follow this sign, or not?

You are hurrying to catch this bus, but find these doors closed, and you cannot get on. Do you hammer on the doors to attract the driver's attention? Explain your answer.

9

You are being taken for a drive in this car
by your French friend.

1. Which road are you travelling along?
2. Are you entering or leaving a
   village?

10

You have arrived at a railway station and
see this office. Is it:

a) the station master's office?
b) the left luggage office?
c) the information office?
d) the seat reservation office?
e) the ticket office?

11

Details of church services are often found on the outskirts of towns on the continent. You see this sign at the roadside as you reach the town of Etaples.

1. Does this sign give details of Protestant or Catholic services?
2. How many services are held on Sundays?
3. At what time is the last one on Sunday?
4. On what other day are services held?
5. Imagine that it is 6.30 p.m. on that day. Are you in time for the service?

12

To which of the following places do these signs direct you?

a) a railway station?
b) a swimming pool?
c) an information office?
d) a car park?
e) a bus stop?

13

You are walking along the pavement and want to cross the road at a busy junction. Do you cross at this sign now, or do you wait?

14

The driver of the car you are in is looking for somewhere to park, and this side road looks convenient. Does this sign suggest that there would be any objection, or not? Explain your answer.

15

You are going along a road when you see this notice indicating a track specially provided for certain road users. Would you use it if you were:

    a)   cycling?
    b)   riding a horse?
    c)   driving a car?
    d)   walking?
    e)   riding a motor bike?

16

You are shopping, and come across this display. What are you looking at?

    a)   paint
    b)   soap powder
    c)   coffee
    d)   dog food
    e)   solid fuel

PISTE CYCLABLE PRIORITAIRE

17

You see this sign as you are approaching the crossroads in a car. Just before you reach it, a man riding along the cycle track crosses the road in front of you. You brake sharply to avoid hitting him. Who is in the wrong?

PASSAGE PROTÈGÈ

18

At the crossroads, should you give way to a car approaching from the right, or are you allowed to go straight on?

ville propre

ville accueillante

19

While you are walking in the street you come across this box fixed to the wall of a building.
1. What should you put into this box?
2. How are the people of this town persuaded to make use of it?

UN
GRAND
CHOIX
DE
COLLANTS

die
3,50 et 5,00

belami

6,00

BOMO

6,50 et 7,00

20

You are walking around a supermarket and see this display rack.
1. What is on sale in the rack?
2. Would you expect to find many different makes, sizes and styles?
3. Write down the price of 'belami' in words.

You are carrying a lot of luggage and need a taxi. Should you wait by this notice, or should you go to the other end of the taxi rank?

TAXIS
TÊTE DE
STATION

22

As you are driving along a busy road you notice this sign.

1. What is the kangaroo telling you to do?
2. What is the driver telling you to do?
3. What is the French for 'road safety'?

ROULEZ MOINS VITE...

ATTACHEZ-VOUS

SÉCURITÉ

dsr DÉLÉGATION A LA SÉCURITÉ ROUTIÈRE

This is the outside of an important building.

1. Is it:
   a) a railway station?
   b) a supermarket?
   c) an indoor market?
   d) a public swimming bath?
   e) a sorting office?

23

2. What do you understand by the initials S.N.C.F?

3. Who is supposed to use the doorway on the left?
4. What is the purpose of the object on the pedestal, on the left-hand side of the picture?

P

SNCF

DEPART

LIMITE 30

BOITE AUX LETTRES

24

A sign like this is likely to be found in many French towns. Draw the outline of the sign and fill in the information in English, in the same order as it appears on the photograph. Use the following terms:

furnished flats
camp site
garages
restaurants
tourists' information office
youth hostel
shows
hotels

25

Your coach driver wants to park near some toilets. Is he allowed to pull into this lay-by? Give the reason for your answer.

26

This notice stands behind a fence by the roadside.

1. Where is the café?
2. What may you do if you want a meal there?

27

This is the rear window of a Renault car.
Is the driver in the car behind requested:

    a)   to overtake?

    b)   to keep his distance?

    c)   to stop?

    d)   to make a note of the E L F advertisement on the right?

    e)   not to travel too fast?

28

You have pulled in at a B.P. garage.

    1.   How much will you have to pay for 14 litres of petrol?

    2.   Who operates this petrol pump?

29

1. What are the two purposes of the shelter?
2. Should you park your car by the shelter at any time? Give the reason for your your answer

30

You might see this notice on a door if you were staying at a camping and caravan site.

1. What is a WC?
2. What is forbidden?

31

1. Which of the following items can you buy in this shop according to the words above the windows?
   a) pancakes c) eggs
   b) cheese   d) flour
                e) salt
                f) butter
2. Outside the door, you can see a lot of containers. Are the contents most likely to be:
   a) water?
   b) paint?
   c) milk?
   d) gas?
   e) paraffin?
3. What is the equivalent of this shop in this country?

32

While you are out for a walk you see this warning sign. It is intended particularly for motorists.

1. Further along the road, nearer the bridge, you meet some boys who want to pitch their tent by the river for the night. What should you tell them?
2. Are you fairly near the mouth of the river at this point? Give the reason for your answer.

33

1. Is the white car illegally parked? How do you know?
2. 'Stat' is an abbreviation. Write the word in full.

34

This shop window attracts your attention.
1. What is probably the best buy in the shop? Give your reason.
2. What sort of glove do you imagine is on sale here?
3. You decide to buy two hand towels and two gloves at the shop. How much will you have to pay altogether?
4. Do you think that the prices advertised are normal or reduced?

35

You are at a fairground and notice this vehicle.
1. What is advertised on the vehicle?
2. What is the name of the vehicle owner?
3. Where does he live?

36

This warning sign is displayed prominently at the side of the road.

1. Is it intended for the motorist, or for the pedestrian?
2. What is the danger?
3. How can the danger be avoided?
4. Over what distance does the danger last?

DANGER
RALENTIR
CHAUSSEE·DEFORMEE
SUR 200 M

37

This timetable is displayed at the bus station. 'Transports Citroën' is the name of a bus company.

1. From which town do the buses set out?
2. Where should you go to book a seat on one of these buses?
3. You want to get to Montreuil in time for the morning market. At what time does your bus leave?
4. See how many of the destinations mentioned you can find on a map of North East France.

TRANSPORTS CITROËN
DÉPARTS DE BERCK

DIRECTION DE						
AIRE ½ LA LYS	6ʰ50					
ARMENTIERES	6ʰ50					
BETHUNE						
BRUAY						
HESDIN						
LILLE						
MERVILLE	6ʰ50				16ʰ15	
MONTREUIL	6ʰ50				16ʰ15	
STPOL			12ʰ10	13ʰ	16ʰ15	17ʰ35
					16ʰ15	

LOCATION DES PLACES ICI

Camping Caravaning
de la mer
TOUT CONFORT
. PISCINE CHAUFFEE
. TENNIS
. SPORTS ET JEUX
. ACCES DIRECT A LA MER
◄ Ste CECILE-PLAGE ◄

38

This board advertises a nearby camp site.

1. Why do you think the camp site at Ste Cécile is called 'Camping Caravaning de la mer'?
2. What are the advantages of camping here?

39

This notice is found at the entrance to a public garden.

1. Under what circumstances would one not be allowed to enter?
2. What is the penalty for breaking the regulation?

L'ACCÉS DU JARDIN EST INTERDIT AUX CHIENS SOUS PEINE D'AMENDE

Tout pour la Future Maman et le Bébé
Caprice Natal

LAYETTE • PUERICULTURE   Caprice Natal

40

1. What is the name of this shop?
2. Which of the following items would you expect to be able to buy here?
   a) a baby's cot
   b) a shirt for a boy of 15
   c) nappies
   d) a potted plant
   e) a pair of shoes for your father

41

This is an advertisement for a well known hovercraft service.

1. Where does this hovercraft service operate from?
2. To which country does it take passengers?
3. How is travelling by Hoverlloyd made to seem attractive?

This photograph shows the interior of a supermarket. According to the notices suspended from the ceiling, what is on sale in this part of the shop?

42

This sign stands at a road junction on the outskirts of a small town.

1. Which town are you in?
2. What is to be found in the direction indicated by the arrow?
3. What is the name of the road?

43

44

You arrive at a railway station and see this machine in the entrance hall.

1. What sort of ticket does the machine dispense?
2. How do you obtain a ticket from the machine?
3. Why do you think the word 'française' appears on the notice?

45

This board gives details of trains leaving this station.

1. You want to go to Paris. Which platform should you go to?
2. The information on the left-hand side of the board is only partly visible. What would it tell you if you could see it all?
3. How do you get from this platform to the one opposite, without crossing the lines?

46

These two signs direct you to two different buildings.

1. From which period in history does the citadel date?
2. To which organisation must you belong if you wish to make use of the other building?

47

1. What is the name of this shop?
2. Which of the following would you expect to buy here?
    a) a garden chair
    b) a bed
    c) a typewriter
    d) a shrub
    e) a book
    f) a table

This petrol pump delivers two grades of **48**
petrol.
  1. Which grades of petrol can you buy
      at the pump?
  2. Which series of figures, top, middle
      or bottom, tells you:
      a) the price of petrol?
      b) how much petrol you have taken?
      c) how much you have to pay for
         the actual quantity taken?

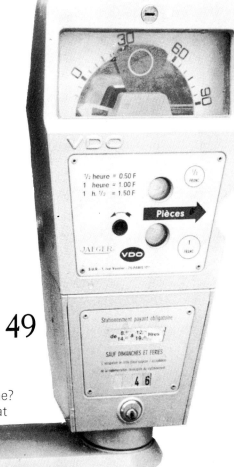

You have just driven up beside this French parking **49**
meter.
  1. What is the longest period of time you may
      park at this meter?
  2. How much does it cost for that length of time?
  3. If you wished to park for a shorter time, what
      choice of time have you?

50

You are walking along the street when you see these two signs.

1. To which important places do they show the way?
2. What is in the canister on the pavement, near the man with his dog?

These notices are found on the roadside in the nearby forest. Hardelot is a resort on the north coast of France.

1. Is this forest public or private property?
2. For which purpose is it suggested that you might go along this forest road?

51

3. Which two precautions should you take when you are in the forest?

52

You have arrived at a camp site and stop to read this board displayed outside.

1. Write out in French what F.F.C.C. stands for.
2. Why should you expect to find adequate facilities at this camp site?

53

This 'No Entry' sign is not far from the entrance of a castle open to the public.

1. Are you more likely to find this sign inside or outside the castle?
2. Is this sign a request or an order?
3. For whom is the sign intended?

You see these signs on the corner of a building at a road junction.

1. Copy from the sign the French names of two places which are concerned with law enforcement.
2. Copy from the sign the French names of two places which are concerned with health.
3. How far away is the car park?
4. Would you go along this road in search of:
   a) a telephone? b) a car club?
   c) a priest?
   d) a tourists' information bureau?
   e) a bus station?

54

This notice is fixed to a concrete pole at the road-side.

1. What risk do you run if you climb the pole?
2. What is the purpose of the pole?

This is the window of a shop selling clothes.

1. Would you necessarily pay the price shown in the window for the roll-neck shirts?

Give the reason for your answer. 2. Are the men's casual shirts 'seconds', sale-quality or best quality? 3. How much could you pay for the blouses?

This poster is publicising a fair.
1. For how many days was the fair open to the general public?
2. When was the fair especially open to businessmen?
3. Which countries were responsible for organising the fair?
4. In which town would you have visited the fair?

58

You notice this car parked as you are crossing the road.
1. To whom does it belong?
2. What would someone be most likely to visit these premises for?
3. What is the poster in the main window advertising?

You are doing the shopping for your family. **59**
This is your shopping list:

    loaf of bread
    torch battery
    roast chicken
    6 slices garlic sausage
    cylinder camping gas
    250 grammes frying steak
    2 kilogrammes new potatoes
    1 litre milk

Which of these items are you likely to get on this street, judging by the signs you can see?

On 20th April you are driving along a road looking for somewhere to stop for a picnic. You see these signs

1. Which three things are forbidden along this stretch of the grass verge today.
2. What is special about Avenue Godin, Avenue Dune aux Loups and Avenue Canche?

60

You are in town, and have several things to do: Which of the following things is it possible to do in these two buildings?
- a) cash some travellers' cheques
- b) buy some fishing tackle
- c) have a meal
- d) buy some shellfish
- e) insure your luggage for the rest of your holiday

62

61 You are about to board this bus. You are visiting this town and have no ticket of any sort.
1. Which of the two doors facing you do you use when getting on?
2. When is the other door used?
3. Find out the difference between 'tickets' and 'billets'.

You have lost your socks and need to buy a new pair.
You stop to see if this shop has what you want.

1. Are children's or adults' clothes on display here?
2. Which garments are displayed? Are there any socks?
3. Do you think that you would be welcome to go in and look around, and try on some of the clothes? How do you know?
4. Which item is available in all sizes?
5. Which items of clothing here are your size?

This sign is at a village bus stop where you are waiting for a bus to Le Touquet.

1. It is 1 p.m. How long will you have to wait for your bus?
2. Can you change your mind, and go to Boulogne on the same bus?
3. When is there a special bus service to a market?
4. Where is the market?
5. To which towns are there special buses on school days?
6. What advice is given to people who wish to catch the bus at this stop?

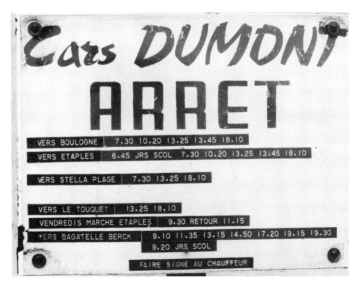

65

1. Which of the following items could you buy at the shop?
   a) stamps
   b) cigarettes
   c) souvenirs
   d) money orders
   e) newspapers
   f) notepaper and envelopes
   g) paperbacks
   h) suntan lotion
2. Which types of entertainment can you see advertised?
3. What is the meaning of the sign sticking out above the shop door? You will see this sign all over France.

66

Both posters are publicising the same type of attraction.

1. What is the attraction?
2. When and where did both events take place? Give as much detail as you can.
3. France Inter is the French equivalent of Radio 1. In what way was France Inter involved?
4. Say what you think 'Trinity' and 'Crazy Horse' are.

67

This shop is on a corner, opposite a friend's house.

1. What can you buy in the shop?
2. Where does the side street on the left lead?

68

1. What evidence is there that these cars are parked on the correct side of the street?
2. What sort of a place is 'La Flambée'?

69

You are walking down this street on the way to the town centre.

1. What service can you obtain at this chemist's shop, in addition to the usual ones?
2. Can people staying at the hotel eat there if they wish? Explain the reason for your answer.

70

1. What is the large building facing you at the end of the street?
   a) a railway station
   b) a bus station
   c) a town hall
   d) a post office
   e) an hotel
2. Why are there no cars parked on the other side of the road?
3. Is parking restricted here every day of the week, or not?
4. What sort of parking restrictions are imposed in a 'zone bleue'?

1.   Is this lady most likely to have just:
     a) posted a parcel?   b) visited a sick relative?   c) bought some stamps?
     d) cashed a cheque?   e) reported a theft?
2.   Are the clothes in the shop window for boys, men, women or girls?
3.   In addition to clothes, which of the following things can you buy in this shop?
     sweets   sheets   cuff links
     tablecloth   screwdriver   tennis balls

1.   Which petrol is on sale at this service
     station?
2.   Copy the information on the main
     display board in French, in the
     same order as it appears below.
          air for tyres
          car wash
          diesel
          lubrication
          two-stroke mixture
          tyre repairs
3.   This garage is an agency for which
     make of car?

73

You come across this doorway in the main street of a town.

1. Why would a person come to these offices?
2. When would you find them open?
   a) Monday, 11 a.m.
   b) Saturday morning
   c) Wednesday, 3 p.m.
   d) Friday, 2 p.m.
   e) Tuesday, 9.30 a.m.

CAISSE D'EPARGNE
ENTREE PROVISOIRE

BUREAUX OUVERTS
LE LUNDI DE 14.30 A 17H
DU MARDI AU VENDREDI
DE 9 A 12.30 ET DE 14.30 A 17H
LE SAMEDI DE 9 A 12.30

1. Over what distance is the 'No Parking' sign valid?
2. Are you approaching, or have you just passed some road works?
3. Who owns the business?
4. What is the full address of the Head Office of this firm?

74

INTERDIT
SUR TOUTE LA LONGUEUR

JL
11 B^d Jean Mermoz
NEUILLY (Seine)

FIN
DE TRAVAUX

ENTREPRISE
JEAN LEFEBVRE

75

This type of shop is called an 'Alimentation Générale'. A lorry is delivering bottles at the moment.

1. Do the crates on the lorry contain bottles of:
   - a) lemonade?
   - b) wine?
   - c) beer?
   - d) mineral water?
   - e) fruit juice?
2. What is the brand name of this drink?
3. Name the types of drink which you can see advertised as being on sale.
4. Name the types of food which you can see advertised as being on sale.
5. What is an 'Alimentation Générale'?

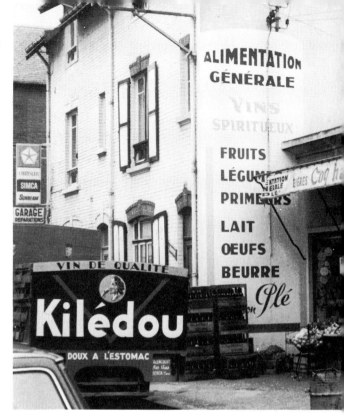

76

This sign marks the boundary of the town of Le Touquet.

1. In which seasons is Le Touquet recommended for a relaxing week-end?
2. Le Touquet is publicised as a particular type of resort. Which type?
3. What are drivers requested to do? And by whom?

These signs are at the entrance to a camp site.
1. Where is the reception office?
2. What do you have to do at the reception office?
3. Who would keep to the right of this notice board?

These posters advertise two different places in the region.
1. Which two places are advertised?
2. How far away by car is the place advertised at the top?
3. Is it a large or small place?
4. Cucq is a village. How would you get there by car, according to the poster?
5. In the lower advertisement, what would the lady be saying in English?
6. What is the number 62 for, before Audruicq?
7. Audruicq is a name. Try to find out what it is.

These notices are displayed on the door of a historic building which is open to the public.

1. At what times of day is the castle open to the public?
2. Is there a guide to show visitors round?
3. You are English. What is done to help you appreciate the castle?
4. You are in a party of two adults and three children. How much will it cost you to go in?
5. Where is the ticket office?
6. Which added attraction is there during the summer season?

CITADELLE
CHATEAU ROYAL

DU XII ᴱ AU XVII ᴱ

OUVERTURE   9ᴴ30 A 12ᴴ00
              14ᴴ00 A 19ᴴ00

VISITE COMMENTEE PAR BANDE MAGNETIQUE

THE VISIT IS COMMENTED IN ENGLISH

BESCHREIBUNG ᴅᴇʀ FESTUNG ᴀᴜᴄʜ ᴀᴜꜰ **DEUTSCH**

PRIX D'ENTREE ENFANTS 1ꟳᴿ50 ADULTES 3ꟳᴿOO

BUREAU 3ᴱ PORTE A DROITE

DU **27 MAI** ᴀᴜ **31 AOUT**

ENFANTS ꟳᴿ   DE **21**ᴴ A **24**ᴴ   ADULTES ꟳᴿ

PROMENADE NOCTURNE

ILLUMINATIONS
AMBIANCE

CAFÉ-BRASSERIE
Aux Amis du Douaisis

Steack Frites 6,50
Moules   "   6,00
Poulet   "   6,50
Omelette   "   6,00
Jambon   "   6,50
Saucisses "   5,50
service non compris

This board is on the pavement outside a café. You have been hitch-hiking and decide to stop here for something to eat.

1. You can only afford the cheapest meal. What would you get?
2. If you could only afford six francs for something to eat, would you choose mussels or ham?
3. If you ordered chicken, how much would it cost you?
4. What would you have to pay for in addition to the food and drink?
5. Write down the name of this café-brasserie, as though you were making a note for future reference.
6. What is served with each dish?
7. Is there an egg dish on the menu?
8. You are very hungry and would like a four-course meal. Would you go in?

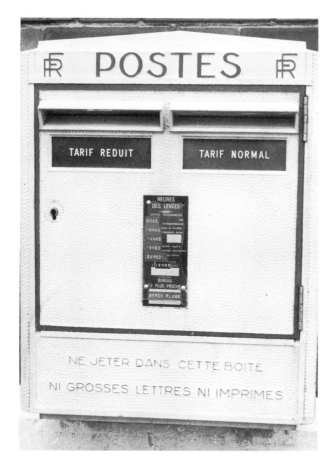

81

This is a French post box. There is a two-class postal system in France.

1. Which opening in this posting box is for first class mail, and which opening is for second class mail? Explain how you know.
2. Which of the following items should you not post in this box?
   a) a postcard?
   b) a bulky letter
   c) a birthday card
   d) a newspaper
   e) a magazine

82

You would like a quick snack, and you see this information in a café window.

1. How are all the items on the list served?
2. If you were a vegetarian, which item in the list would you choose?
3. Which of the items in the list would you ask for in French if you wanted:
   a) potted minced pork?
   b) liver pâté?
   c) rabbit pâté
   d) garlic sausage?
   e) cooked ham?

83

This list displayed outside a café shows the minimum price which can be charged for certain items.

1. Do the prices include the cost of the service?
2. What would you pay for two cups of coffee?
3. What would you pay for a litre of lemonade?
   How many glasses would that be?
4. What would a glass of beer cost?
5. What else can you buy?

84

You are passing this shop window and see some clothes hanging up.

1. Are the clothes for sale?
2. What does it cost for jackets and trousers?
3. What could you have done for 5 francs?
4. What could you have done for 8 francs?
5. Describe the qualities of the service here.

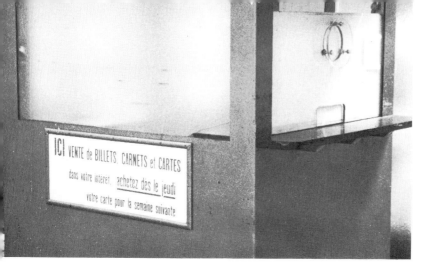

ICI VENTE de BILLETS, CARNETS et CARTES

dans votre intérêt, achetez dès le jeudi

votre carte pour la semaine suivante

This notice is fixed to a kiosk at a bus terminus.

1. Why would bus travellers come to the kiosk?
2. What are people, who travel to work every day by bus, advised to do?

The Bineau company owns this delivery van.

1. What does the company specialise in?
2. With which of the following would you say that the Bineau company is also concerned?
   a) television installation
   b) building
   c) interior decorating
   d) beach wear
   e) garden landscaping

Le spécialiste de la moquette

Ent BINEAU.F

REVETEMENTS° SOLS et MURS

PEINTURE · VITRERIE

69 rue de la Mer
BERCK·PLAGE tel 169

ENCADREMENTS

87

Your pen-friend's father used to work here.

1. What happened to these offices?
2. When?
3. How are prospective customers reassured?

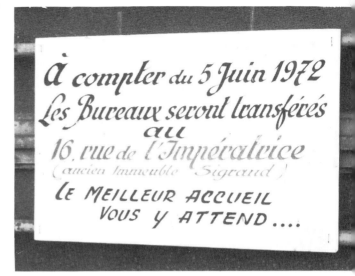

à compter du 5 Juin 1972
Les Bureaux seront transférés
au
16. rue de l'Impératrice
(ancien Immeuble "Sigrand")

LE MEILLEUR ACCUEIL
VOUS Y ATTEND ....

88

You are at a level crossing, and see these two notices.

1. What should you do before crossing the railway lines?
2. Why should you follow these instructions?

NE TRAVERSEZ PAS
sans REGARDER dans les
DEUX DIRECTIONS
Un train peut en
CACHER un autre

UN TRAIN PEUT
EN CACHER
UN AUTRE

89

This notice is found at the entrance to a large parking space.

1. Where is this parking area situated?
2. If you were visiting this town by car, could you park in this area?

Dry cleaning and washing are available at this launderette. You have a pair of trousers and a skirt for dry cleaning.

1. What will that service cost?
2. What weight of clothes must not be exceeded at that price?

You also have some washing — about 10 lbs. of clothes.

3. What will it cost to get them washed and dried?
4. Will you have to pay extra for soap, or anything else?
5. How long will it take to dry your washing?

90

91

This notice is displayed on the fruit and vegetable counter of a supermarket.

1. Which fruits can be bought here?
   a) pears b) apples c) bananas d) plums e) cherries
2. Which vegetables can be bought here?
   a) leeks b) potatoes c) cabbages d) carrots e) lettuce
3. How much would you have to pay for:
   a) 1 kilo of apples?   b) 2 kilos of carrots?
4. Are the prices quoted normal or reduced? How do you know?
5. Which nuts can be bought at this counter?

92

PAR ARRETE PREFECTORAL
et par mesure d'hygiene

l'accès du magasin est interdit
aux animaux
même tenus en laisse

You see this notice at the entrance to a shop. Your French friend is about to go into the shop, and he has his dog with him.

1. Is he allowed to take the dog in on a lead?
2. What reason is given for this law?
3. What sort of shop do you think it is?
4. Is the law made by the management of the shop, or is it an official law?

93 Here is a public telephone outside a post office. Look carefully at the instructions on the box.

   1. What coins would you need to make a call using this telephone?
   2. What should you do after putting the money in?
   3. How can you find out how to make an inter-city call?
   4. Which number should you dial: a) to make a complaint?
       b) to ask for information? c) to call the police?
       d) to send a telegram?
       e) to contact the fire brigade?

94 Look at the shop next to the café.

   1. Which of the following items can be purchased there?
       a) a writing pad
       b) a transistor radio
       c) cups
       d) a leather diary cover
       e) books
       f) a television set
       g) an electric plug
       h) a note book
       i) a sewing machine
       j) a rubber
   2. Which service is provided while you wait?
   3. What is the purpose of the blackboard outside the shop?

1. The address of Alain Deleplace's business is not included in the advertisement. Explain where his shop is to be found.
2. What is he the local agent for?
3. What sort of equipment would you expect to see on display in his shop?
4. 'Bagatelle' is the name of a park. What sort of park is it?
5. What amenities are there in the park for refreshment?
6. Write down the name of the hotel which appears on the advertisement hoarding.
7. What is its telephone number?
8. What is particularly attractive about the swimming pools at the Saint-Hubert camping ground?
9. What sort of an agency is 'Corbasson'?

96

You want to send five letters costing 50 centimes each. Here is a stamp machine.

1. Can you get exactly five stamps?
2. What coins do you need to obtain your stamps?
3. Would you press the button below the slot in order to get your stamps? Give the reason for your answer.

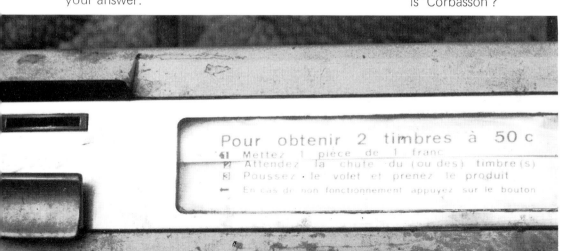

Pour obtenir 2 timbres à 50 c
1) Mettez 1 pièce de 1 franc
2) Attendez la chute du (ou des) timbre (s)
3) Poussez le volet et prenez le produit
— En cas de non fonctionnement appuyez sur le bouton

Imagine that you spent a short holiday at Le Touquet from the 14th to the 22nd April, 1973.

1. Which two special events took place during that week?
2. Which other activities and entertainments were available for you? Which places in Le Touquet might visitors reach by taking the Avenue Vincent?
4. Which sort of vehicles have to use Avenue Vincent?

You are at this post office at 6.30 p.m.

1. It is Friday. Is the office open?
2. When will the office be open tomorrow?

It is Monday, the 13th July.

3. When is the office open today?
4. Will you be able to buy some stamps?
5. How do you know that the post office will be open tomorrow?
6. Will you be able to collect a letter left for you?
7. Will you be able to send a telegram from this office?

It is Sunday. You arrive here at noon.

8. Is the office open?

98

Rennes – R.P. – HEURES d'OUVERTURE :		
JOURS	**HORAIRES**	**OPÉRATIONS**
1°) JOURS ORDINAIRES (du LUNDI au VENDREDI)	8 h. à 19 h.	TOUTES OPÉRATIONS
	TÉLÉGRAPHE & TÉLÉPHONE	
le SAMEDI fermeture à 12 h.	8 h. à 12 h.	TOUTES OPÉRATIONS
2°) DIMANCHES et JOURS FÉRIÉS	8 h. à 11 h.	POSTE RESTANTE & INSTANCES sauf CONTRE-REMBOURSEMENTS
	8 h. à 12 h.	TÉLÉGRAPHE - TÉLÉPHONE VENTE de TIMBRES-POSTE au DÉTAIL
3°) JOURS CHÔMÉS PONTS	8 h. à 12 h.	TOUTES OPÉRATIONS
PONTS entre un DIMANCHE & un JOUR FÉRIÉ		

You are in the Co-op and are looking out for some special offers.

1. 'Skip' is a washing powder. In what sort of container is it sold?
2. This store markets its own brand of certain items. Name two which are advertised in the photograph, and state the prices.

You are spending the Christmas holidays in Boulogne. You are outside the post office and have two letters to post. It is 10.30 a.m. on Friday.

1. You have:
   a) a letter for Calais. What time will it go?
   b) a first class letter for Ireland. Should you put it into the right- or left-hand box?
2. You have forgotten a letter for England. How late can you leave it if you want it to go today?
3. How many times will these post boxes be cleared on New Year's Day?

100

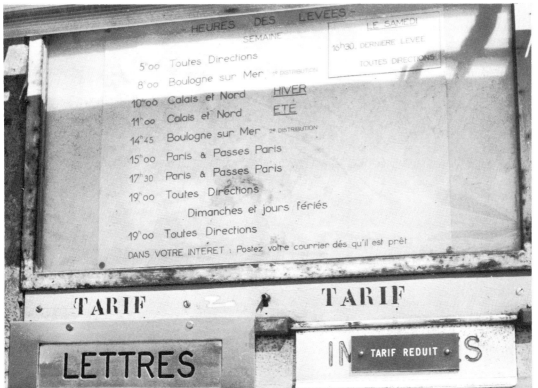

SOUSCRIVEZ DES MAINTENANT

ANANAS
COTE D'IVOIRE
10 tranches entières
boîte 570 g

2^f**10**

PETITS POIS
COOP très fins
lot 3 boîtes 4/4

4^f**90**

BISCUITS
CHOCO
LES BONS COPAINS
le paquet

1^f**50**

CHOCOLAT
A CROQUER
COOP 5 x 100 g

3^f**20**

101

1. What is the name of this shop?
2. Name one commodity sold in:
   a) packets b) tins c) 100 gramme pieces
3. Is the pineapple sold in chunks or slices?
4. How much does the pineapple cost?

FIN
DE ZONE
BLEUE

TOLERIE CARROSSERIE
PEINTURE JEANNESSON
DEPANNAGE
Rue de l'Est . BERCK ☎ 238

ASSURANCES toutes branches
Cabinet J. BLIN
Prêts SOVAC pour Acheter... Construire...
Crédit automobile
35, r. du Docteur Danvin · Berck · tél. 627

AFFICHAGE MUNICIPAL   AMC
95 SANNOIS

CONCHIL-LE-TEMPLE
(près de BERCK)
DIMANCHE 20 MAI 1973
AUTO-CROSS
INTERNATIONAL

CONCHIL-LE-TEMPLE
(près de BERCK)
DIMANCHE 20 MAI 1973
AUTO-CROSS
INTERNATIONAL

STATION
DU PNEU
R. CAUCHETEUX

STATION
DU PNEU
R. CAUCHETEUX

Berck-sur-Mer — Salle des Fêtes
Dimanche 22 Avril 1973. a 21 h.
BAL DE LA MUSIQUE
JAN
ALAIN

102

1. What kind of business does Jeannesson run?
2. Which sport is advertised?
3. Where did it take place?
4. What services does J. Blin offer?
5. Explain the importance of the disc above the left-hand side of the board.
6. When did the advertised dance take place?

```
        → ENTREES ←

SALADE DE TOMATES        1f20
ŒUF EN GELEE             1 50
CORNET DE JAMBON         1f00
SALADE NICOISE           2 00
TOMATES MURCY            1f 0
BARQUETTE DE MOULES      1  0
ASSIETTE DE CRUDITES     1f 0
FILETS DE HARENG         1 50
RILLETTES MAISON
TERRINE MAISON
MUSEAU VINAIGRETTE  2 00
ASSIETTE DE CHARCUTERIE 2 00
COQUILLE ST JACQUES
TOURTE DE FRUITS DE MER

    _ PLATS DE RESISTANCE _ ←
POULET MAYONNAISE        4f50

ROTI DE PORC EN GELEE    5f50
ROTI DE VEAU FROID       5f50
ASSIETTE ANGLAISE        6 00
STEACK GRILLE FRITES     6 50
ANDOUILLETTE CHABLIS
COTE DE PORC MAISON      4f50
CHOUCROUTE ALSACIENNE 6f50

OTRE SELECTION DE FROMAGES

    _ NOS DESSERTS _

ANANAS AU KIRSCH         2f00
COUPE DE FRUITS
GLACES AU CHOIX
```

103

You have decided to have a meal at this restaurant.

1. How much would you have to pay if you ate tomato salad, cold roast veal, and ice cream?
2. How much would this meal cost if a 15% service charge was added?
3. How much would you pay for a meal consisting of scallops, a selection of slices of various cold meats, and pineapple?
4. How much would this meal cost if the service charge was set at 10%?
5. What is the price of herring fillets, followed by chicken, followed by fruit cup?
6. How many courses could you have at this restaurant?
7. What are the equivalent names of these courses in English?

104

You are at a level crossing provided with a telephone.

1. Why would you have to use this telephone?
2. How long should you wait before using it?
3. How do you make a telephone call from this box?
4. Write down in French what you should say into the mouthpiece.
5. Write down in English the gist of the message.
6. What is the purpose of the map?
7. Whereabouts on the map are you supposed to be?

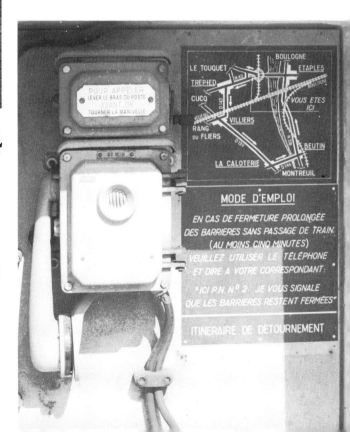

1. You have a very urgent letter to post, and it is 4 p.m. on Saturday. **105**
Do you:
   a) post it here immediately?
   b) wait until Sunday?
   c) go to the nearest post office?
2. At which town is the nearest post office?
3. How often is this box emptied at the weekend?
4. How often is it emptied on each other day of the week?

HEURES
DES LEVEES

JOURS OUVRABLES

9H30
11H50
14H00
18H00
SAMEDI
15H45

Les correspondances pour la localité déposées avant

seront, sauf le samedi, distribuées le jour même.

NCHES ERIES

BUREAU
LE PLUS PROCHE

. BERCK . PLAGE .

RECEPTION
ET
RENSEIGNEMENT
SONNER ici
S.V.P

LES CHIENS EN LIBERTÉ
SONT FORMELLEMENT
INTERDITS.

LES CHIENS
EN LIBERTE
SONT INTERDITS

LES DÉPARTS
DOIVENT ÊTRE
FAITS AVANT 12h

LE TÉLÉPHONE
EST OUVERT DE
9 À 11. ET DE
15 A 18.

BUREAU

106

This is the reception office at a camping caravan site.

1. If there was nobody in the office, what would you do to gain atten
2. When are you allowed to use the telephone in the office?
3. What is forbidden on the camp si
4. When your stay at the site is over at what time of day must you vac your plot?

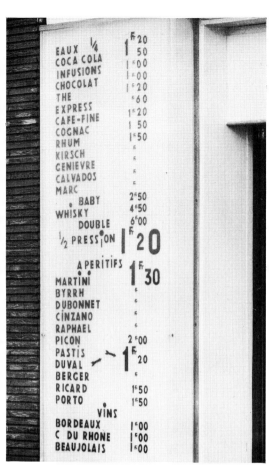

EAUX ¼	1F20	
	50	
COCA COLA	1F00	
INFUSIONS	1F00	
CHOCOLAT	1F20	
THE	F60	
EXPRESS	1F20	
CAFE-FINE	1 50	
COGNAC	1F50	
RHUM	F	
KIRSCH	F	
GENIEVRE	F	
CALVADOS	F	
MARC	F	
BABY	2F50	
WHISKY	4F50	
DOUBLE	6F00	
½ PRESSION	1F20	
APERITIFS	1F30	
MARTINI		
BYRRH	F	
DUBONNET	F	
CINZANO	F	
RAPHAEL	F	
PICON	2F00	
PASTIS	1F20	
DUVAL		
BERGER		
RICARD	1F50	
PORTO	1F50	
VINS		
BORDEAUX	1F00	
C DU RHONE	1F00	
BEAUJOLAIS	1F00	

107

You are with a group of adults and children. You have ordered some drinks and want to work out the cost so that you can check the bill. Do not forget that there is a 10% service charge. Here are the drinks you ordered:

a) a glass of wine
b) a glass of draught beer
c) a cup of tea
d) a glass of mineral water
e) a soft drink
f) a cup of coffee (say which one)
g) a glass of brandy
h) an aperitif (say which one)

1. How much does your order come to?
2. How much change should you receive from 15 francs?

108

1. What is the purpose of this instrument?
2. Explain in detail how you should make the instrument work.

You are coming out of the supermarket.
1. What do you think is the purpose of the label 'client suivant'?
2. What are you asked to do at the check-out?
3. Is this a particularly polite request?

109 Having studied the notice outside, you go into this restaurant for a meal.
1. Where is the dining room?
2. You are with two friends. You choose the menu of the day, and your friends choose steak and chips, and rib of pork. How much does the meal come to, including the service charge?
3. The four people at the next table are eating sausages, mussels, ham and omelette. How much do they pay altogether for the meal, including the service charge?
4. Which of these items can you buy here to take away?
   a) sandwiches
   b) wine
   c) chips
   d) hot dogs

TOPICS

The following is a list of general topic headings under which the photographs may be classified. The + sign indicates that the photograph relates to more than one topic. The numbers refer to the photograph numbers in the text.

Accommodation 68+, 46+
Bus travel 8, 29+, 37, 61, 64, 70+, 85, 89+
Café/Restaurant 26, 80, 82, 83, 103, 107, 109
Caisse d'Épargne 73
Camp site 3, 4, 30, 38+, 52, 77, 106
Castle visit 79
Church services 11
Garage 28, 48, 72
Litter 19
Parking 23+, 25, 29+, 33, 49, 60+, 68+, 70+, 74+, 89+, 102+
Personal danger 55
Post 23+, 81, 96, 98, 100, 105
Public garden 39
Publicity 22, 35, 38+, 41, 57, 58, 65+, 66, 74+, 75+, 76, 78, 86, 95, 97+, 102+
Railway 10, 23+, 44, 45, 88, 104+
Removal of premises 87
Road signs 7, 9+, 12, 13, 14, 15, 43, 46+, 50, 53, 54, 60+
Road signs (information) 5+, 17+, 18+, 24, 51, 74+, 97+
Road signs (warning) 2, 5+, 9+, 17+, 18+, 32, 36
Shops (exterior) 1, 31, 34, 40, 47, 56, 59, 62, 63, 65+, 67, 69, 71, 75+, 84, 90, 94
Shops (interior) 16, 20, 42, 91, 92, 99, 101, 110
Taxi 21
Telephone 29+, 93, 104+
Telescope 108

TOPICS

The following is a list of general topic headings under which the photographs may be classified. The + sign indicates that the photograph relates to more than one topic. The numbers refer to the photograph numbers in the text.

Accommodation 68+, 46+
Bus travel 8, 29+, 37, 61, 64, 70+, 85, 89+
Café/Restaurant 26, 80, 82, 83, 103, 107, 109
Caisse d'Épargne 73
Camp site 3, 4, 30, 38+, 52, 77, 106
Castle visit 79
Church services 11
Garage 28, 48, 72
Litter 19
Parking 23+, 25, 29+, 33, 49, 60+, 68+, 70+, 74+, 89+, 102+
Personal danger 55
Post 23+, 81, 96, 98, 100, 105
Public garden 39
Publicity 22, 35, 38+, 41, 57, 58, 65+, 66, 74+, 75+, 76, 78, 86, 95, 97+, 102+
Railway 10, 23+, 44, 45, 88, 104+
Removal of premises 87
Road signs 7, 9+, 12, 13, 14, 15, 43, 46+, 50, 53, 54, 60+
Road signs (information) 5+, 17+, 18+, 24, 51, 74+, 97+
Road signs (warning) 2, 5+, 9+, 17+, 18+, 32, 36
Shops (exterior) 1, 31, 34, 40, 47, 56, 59, 62, 63, 65+, 67, 69, 71, 75+, 84, 90, 94
Shops (interior) 16, 20, 42, 91, 92, 99, 101, 110
Taxi 21
Telephone 29+, 93, 104+
Telescope 108

WORD LIST

Words which the reader might reasonably be expected to know, or to be able to guess correctly are not included. Meanings given are those appropriate to the context.

abaissez press down, push down
abri shelter
accès access, entry; accès à access to, accès de entry into
accueil welcome, reception
accueillante attractive, welcoming
acheter, achetez buy; achetez dès le jeudi buy as from Thursday
s'adresser apply (for information)
affichage bill-posting, advertising
afin de (d') in order to
ail garlic
aimable kind
alimentation food, foodstuff
allée pathway, lane, avenue
ambiance atmosphere
amende: sous peine d'amende disobedience will be punished by a fine
ameublement furniture, furnishing
ans years
ananas pineapple
ancien former, old
andouillette small pork sausage
annuaire telephone directory
août August
apéritifs drinks taken before a meal, appetisers
appareils apparatus, equipment
appel: numéro d'appel number being telephoned
appeler make a telephone call, ring
apporter bring
appuyez press
arrêt stop
arrêté préfectoral roughly equivalent to a bye-law
assiette anglaise dish of cold meats
assurances insurance
attachez-vous fasten yourself in

attend awaits, is waiting for
attendez wait (for)
attention! look out! take care! (a warning)
auberge de jeunesse youth hostel
auto car
autobus bus
autocar coach, bus
auto-école driving school
automne autumn
automobile car
autre other; un autre another
avant before
avant de before
avec vue normale if you have normal sight
avril April

bain bath
bal dance
bande magnétique tape (recording)
banque bank
baril tub, small barrel
barquette de moules plate of mussels
barrières barriers or gates at a level-crossing
bébé baby
beurre butter
bière beer
bifteack (beef) steak (normally written without an a)
bijoux jewels, jewellery
billet ticket, travel voucher
biscottes rusk-like biscuits, sold in packets
blanchisserie laundry
bleue blue
bocal jar
boissons pilotes list of drinks with their prices, serving as a guide to the minimum prices in force at a particular café

boîte box; tin, can; boîte aux lettres post box

bombe aerosol spray

boucherie butcher's shop

bouillon thin meat soup, which may be served as a drink

boulangerie baker's shop

bouton button, knob

bras du poste receiver arm (of telephone)

brasserie café (alcoholic drinks are on sale)

briochés describes bread made of the same dough as *brioches*

bureau(x) office(s)

cabas shopping bag

cacahuètes peanuts

cacher hide

café coffee

caisses de sortie checkouts (in supermarket)

caisse d'épargne savings bank

Calvados sort of brandy made in Normandy

campagne country (as opposed to town)

cars buses (short form of *autocars*)

carburant fuel for engines

carnets booklets (of tickets)

carrosserie bodywork (of cars)

cartes cards, travel vouchers (usually worth several journeys at reduced fare)

en cas de in the event of, in case of

catch wrestling

cavaliers horse-riders

Chablis name of a dry white wine

charcuterie pork butcher's shop, frequently equivalent to a delicatessen; all forms of meat from pigs

château castle

chauffage central central heating

chauffé(e) heated

chauffeur driver

chaussée déformée uneven road surface

chemin road, way

chemisiers blouses

cher dear, expensive

cheval horse

chiens dogs

chocolat à croquer chocolate (for eating as opposed to cooking)

je choisis I choose

choix choice, selection; au choix choice of . . .

chômés non-working (days)

choucroute a dish from Alsace (cabbage and sausages cooked in wine)

chute: attendez la chute de . . . wait for . . . to drop

cinq five

citadelle citadel, castle

clientèle customers

col neck (of garment)

collants tights

colonie (de vacances) holiday camp for parties of children from school or other organisation

commentée commentated

complet man's suit

composez dial (telephone number)

compris included; service non-compris service charge not included

à compter du . . . with effect from the . . .

comptoir counter, bar

confection making up (of garment); ready-to-wear clothing

confort: tout confort every comfort, a high standard of facilities

construire build, construct

contestations disputes

contre-remboursements cash-on-delivery mail

conventionné: magasin conventionné a shop within a supermarket, but under different ownership, and having an agreement with the supermarket

copains pals, friends, mates

coquilles St-Jacques scallops

cornet de jambon rolled and stuffed slice of ham

correspondances mail, post

correspondant the person to whom you are speaking on the telephone côte rib; coast; **Côte d'Ivoire** Ivory Coast (West African republic); **Côte d'Opale** Channel coast of N.E. France

côté side

courrier mail, post

couverture roofing

crémerie dairy

croquer munch

crudités raw vegetables

cuit cooked

dames ladies

dansante dancing

déformée: **chaussée déformée** uneven road surface

demi half; glass of beer

dépannage emergency breakdown service

départs departures

déposées posted, handed in

dépositaire agent (for a product)

dernière last

dès que (qu') as soon as

au détail retail; in small quantities

détournement detour, action of avoiding

deux two; **les deux** both

diamants diamonds

dimanche Sunday

dire say

directions: **toutes directions** all destinations

distribuées delivered

distribution delivery (postal)

divers various

doivent must

domaniale: **forêt domaniale** state (-owned) forest

don gift

douches showers

draps de bain bath towels

à droite on the right, to the right

durée duration, length of time

eau water; **eaux (minérales)** (mineral) water

école school

écrémé skimmed, skim

église church

emporter take away

en (of it, of them)

encadrements surrounds

endives chicory

enfants children

entières whole

entrée entry, entrance

entrées courses served before the main one in a meal

entreprise business concern, undertaking

entretien maintenance, housewares (in supermarket)

équilibré balanced

essayer try, try on (clothes)

essence petrol, regular grade petrol

étage floor, storey

été summer

êtes (you) are

être (to) be

étui box, carton

éviter avoid

à l'exclusion de(s) to the exclusion of

express espresso coffee

face à face opposite to each other

en face opposite

faciliter make easy

faits made, done, completed

fériés: **jours fériés** holidays

fermées closed

fermeture closing, time of closing

fête foraine travelling fair

feu: **attention au feu** fire risk

filles girls

filtre: **qualité filtre** filter quality (coffee)

fin end

fine liqueur brandy

flacon bottle (possibly plastic)

flaconnages: **petits flaconnages** small bottle sizes

foie liver

foire fair, trade fair

fonctionnement: non fonctionnement failure to work

à fond completely, as far as possible

forêt domaniale state (-owned) forest

formellement strictly, absolutely

formidable tremendous, terrific, fantastic

frites chips

froid cold

fromage cheese

gants (de toilette) gloves (used in place of face-cloth)

garçons boys

gare station

gas oil fuel oil, diesel fuel

géant giant, gigantic

en gelée in jelly (not necessarily fruit jelly)

gendarmerie roughly equivalent to a police station

glaces ice creams

gonflage inflation, blowing up of tyres

graissage greasing, lubrication

grand(e) big

gratuit free, at no charge

gros, grosse(s) large, bulky

hareng herring

haute tension high tension, high voltage

hebdomadaire weekly

heure(s) time(s), hour(s); heures (abbreviated to h.) − o'clock

hippodrome race course (horses)

hiver winter

hommes men

homologué approved, endorsed

horaires time-tables (bus, train)

hôtel de ville town hall

ici here

immeuble block (of flats), Building, House (commercial)

imprimés printed matter (newspapers, magazines, etc.)

incroyable unbelievable, incredible

infusions drinks made in the same way as tea, but with different flavours

inondation flood, flooding

inscrivez-vous register, sign in

instances registered mail for collection at post office

inter et regional long distance calls

Inter: France-Inter French radio station, similar to BBC 1

interdit(e)(s) forbidden, prohibited

intérêt: dans votre intérêt in your (own) interest

introduire insert, put in

itinéraire route

ivoire: Côte d'Ivoire Ivory Coast (West African republic)

jambon ham

jardin garden, park

jeudi Thursday

jeunesse: auberge de jeunesse youth hostel

jeux games

jours days; jours chômés non-working days; jours chômés ponts non-working days between two normal holidays; jours fériés holidays; jours ouvrables working days; jrs scol. school days

journées days

journaux newspapers

juin June

jupes skirts

kirsch sort of brandy

laisse: tenus en laisse (held) on a lead

lait milk

lapin rabbit

laque lacquer

lavage washing

layette baby clothes, baby requirements

légumes vegetables

lentement slowly

lessives washing powders

lettres letters; grosses lettres bulky letters

levée(s) (postal) collection(s)

lever lift, raise

en liberté running loose

librairie bookshop

libre: entrée libre an invitation to come in and look round without obligation

lignes: autocars de lignes service buses

limitée limited

linge linen

literie bedding

location booking, reservation, renting

loisirs: parc de loisirs pleasure ground, amusement park

longueur length

lundi Monday

luxe luxury

lyophilisé specially treated to preserve flavour

magasin shop

mai May

maire mayor

maison house; used to describe a speciality of a restaurant

maman mother, mum

manivelle handle

manteaux coats

marché market; marché commun common market

mardi Tuesday

marée: grande marée very high tide

marinières boiled in water and wine with sliced onion

maroquinerie leather goods

mayonnaise dressing made with eggs, oil etc.

le meilleur the best

mélange 2 temps 2-stroke mixture

même even, same; le jour même the same day

ménagers household

mer sea; fruits de mer sea food

merci thank you

mesdames ladies

messes masses (Catholic church)

mesure: par mesure d'hygiène for reasons of hygiene

mettez put

meubles furniture

meublés furnished flats

mode d'emploi instructions for use

moi me, I

moins less; moins cher cheaper; au moins at least

montée uphill; getting on (bus)

montres watches

moquette fitted carpet

mort death

moules mussels

muguet lily of the valley

en multi-service in individual washing machines

murs walls

museau vinaigrette ox or pig snout with dressing

ne . . . ni . . . ni neither . . . nor

net: prix net price includes service charge

nettoyage à sec dry cleaning

nocturne at night, night-time

noisettes hazel nuts

noix walnuts

nuit dansante dance, evening of dancing

numéro d'appel number being called (telephone)

obtenir obtain

oculaire eye-piece

œufs eggs

opale: Côte d'Opale Channel coast of N.E. France

opérations types of service (post office)

ouvert(s) open

ouverture opening

ouvrables working (days)

pain bread; petit pain small loaf, roll; petits pains briochés rolls made with *brioche* dough

pantalons trousers
papeterie stationery, stationery shop
par by
parler talk, speak
particulier: voitures particulières private cars
à partir de . . . from . . .

passage action of crossing over or going through;
   passage protégé indicates that you have right
   of way at cross roads; passage souterrain
   subway

passés past, beyond
pâté potted meat
pâtisserie cake shop
patronnée supported, patronized

peine: sous peine d'amende disobedience will be
   punished by a fine
peinture painting, paintwork
pénétrer go into
pension de famille boarding house
pépinières nurseries, nursery gardens
perspective view, prospect
petits pois peas
peut can, may
pièce coin
piétons pedestrians
pique-nique picnic
piscine swimming pool
piste cyclable cycle track (beside road)
places seats
plage beach, seaside resort
plat du jour today's special (dish)
plat de résistance main course or dish
plein air open air
plein tarif full fare, normal rate
plomberie plumbing
plus: plus vite quicker
pneus tyres
poids lourds heavy vehicles (buses, lorries)
poignée handle
points spots, dots
poireaux leeks
poissonnerie fishmonger's

polyamide type of man-made fibre
polos casual shirts
pomme apple
pompiers fire-brigade
ponts refers to working days sandwiched
   between two holidays, and which may be
   taken off to make a single longer holiday
porte door
(le)poste post, station, position
(la)poste post office, poste restante service whereby
   letters are kept at the post office for
   collection instead of being delivered
postez post
potable fit to drink
poulet chicken
pour for, in order to
pousser, poussez push
préfectoral of the *préfet*
premier, 1er first
prenez take
près close, near
pression pressure; indicates beer drawn from
   pressurized container
prêt ready
prêts loans
primeurs early vegetables
printemps spring
(nous) prions (we) pray, beg
prioritaire having priority
privé private
prix price, cost; prix net price includes service
   charge
proche: le plus proche nearest
produit product
promenade any sort of travel for pleasure:
   walk, ride, drive etc.
promotionnel: ventes promotionnelles special
   offers (in shops)
propre clean
provisoire provisional, temporary
P.T.T. G.P.O.
puériculture bringing up of children, requirements for children

puissant powerful
pulls sweaters

quai platform
que that

ralentir slow down
rappel reminder
réclamations complaints
réclame special offer (in shop)
récurer scour, clean (pans)
réduit: tarif réduit reduced rate
regarder: sans regarder without looking
régler regulate, adjust
relâcher release
remboursements repayments
renseignements information
réparation repair
repas meal
résistance: plat de résistance main course, dish
   (of meal)
restent remain
retour return
revêtements coverings
rillettes potted mince
robes dresses
rôti roast
rôtisserie roast meat shop
rouges red
roulé: col roulé roll-neck
roulez travel, drive
route road
routier (-ère) road; gare routière bus or coach
   station
rue street

sacs bags
saisons seasons
salade lettuce, green salad; salade niçoise salad
   of eggs, olives, tomatoes, garlic, fish and
   various vegetables
salle room, hall

samedi Saturday
sanitaire sanitation
sans without
saucisse sausage
saucisson sausage
sauf except
savon soap
seau bucket
sec dry; nettoyage à sec dry cleaning
séchage drying
secours help
sécurité safety
self-service cafeteria
semaine week, weekdays
sens direction
sensationnel sensational, fantastic
seront will be
servez-vous serve yourself, help yourself, self
   service
service non compris service charge not included
servies au verre served by the glass
serviettes towels
siècle century
sièges seats
signe: faire signe wave, hold out hand (in order
   to stop bus)
signale inform
site site (historical)
S.N.C.F. Société Nationale des Chemins de Fer
Français (French Railways)
soirée dansante dance, evening of dancing
sols floors
sonner ring (bell)
sortie exit, way out
souterrain: passage souterrain subway
spectacles shows (theatre)
spiritueux spirits (alcoholic)
station resort; station
stationnement parking
suivante following
supermarché supermarket
sur over, for; sur toute la longueur for the whole
   length

surveillance supervision

S.V.P. (s'il vous plaît) please

syndicat d'initiative: S.I., ESSI information
  bureau

tabacs tobacco

tailles sizes

tailleur lady's suit

tampons pads

tarif: plein tarif full fare (on bus); tarif
  normal normal rate, first class post; tarif
  réduit reduced rate, second class post

tasse cup

taxiphone public coin-operated telephone

teinturerie dyeing

tension: haute tension high tension, high
  voltage

tenus held, kept

terrine earthenware pot for cooking potted
  meat; *pâté* cooked in *terrine*

tête head

thé tea (drink)

ticket ticket (but not necessarily the same as
  billet

timbre(s) (poste) (postage) stamp(s)

titre de transport travel voucher, bus pass

tôlerie sheet metalwork

tourner turn

en tournant by turning

tourte covered pie, tart

tout everything

tout, toute, tous, toutes all; tout confort every
  comfort, a high standard of facilities; toutes
  directions all destinations

tranches slices

travaux (road) works

ne traversez pas do not cross

très very

tribunal law court

trop too

utiliser make use of

utilitaires: véhicules utilitaires service vehicles

vaisselle washing-up liquid

variés varied, various

veau veal, meat of calf

véhicules utilitaires service vehicles

vendredi(s) Friday(s)

vente(s) sale(s)

vers to, towards, in the direction of

vestons jackets

veuillez please

vide empty

ville town

vin(s) wine(s)

vinaigrette oil and vinegar dressing

visite visit, tour

vite quick, quickly

vitesse speed,

vitrerie glazing, glasswork

voitures cars

volaille poultry

volet flap, shutter

vouloir: bien vouloir be so kind as to

voyageurs passengers

vue sight

WC water closet, toilet, lavatory

y there

zone bleue central area of town where parking
  is restricted and a special disc has to be
  displayed in one's car